D0903097

Animal Classifications

Reptiles

Angela Royston

heinemann
raintree

© 2015 Heinemann Raintree
an imprint of Capstone Global Library, LLC
Chicago, Illinois

To contact Capstone Global Library, please call
800-747-4992, or visit our web site www.capstonepub.com

All rights reserved. No part of this publication may be
reproduced or transmitted in any form or by any means,
electronic or mechanical, including photocopying,
recording, taping, or any information storage and retrieval
system, without permission in writing from the publisher.

Edited by Helen Cox Cannons, Clare Lewis, and
    Abby Colich
Designed by Steve Mead
Picture research by Tracy Cummins
Production by Victoria Fitzgerald
Originated by Capstone Global Library Ltd
Printed and bound in China by Leo Paper Group

18 17 16 15 14
10 9 8 7 6 5 4 3 2 1

Library of Congress Cataloging-in-Publication Data
Royston, Angela, 1945- author.
  Reptiles / Angela Royston.
    pages cm.—(Animal classification)
  Summary: "This fascinating series takes a very simple
look at animal classifications, with each book focusing on a
different group of animal. This book is about reptiles: what
they do, how they behave, and how these characteristics
are different from other groups of animals. Beautifully
illustrated with colorful photographs, the book shows
many examples of different types of reptiles in their natural
environment."—Provided by publisher.
  Includes bibliographical references and index.
  ISBN 978-1-4846-0754-1 (hb)—ISBN 978-1-4846-0761-9
(pb)—ISBN 978-1-4846-0798-5 (ebook) 1. Reptiles—Juvenile
literature. 2. Animals—Classification—Juvenile literature.
I. Title.

QL644.2.R695 2015
597.9—dc23   2014013464

**This book has been officially leveled by using the F&P
Text Level Gradient™ Leveling System.**

Acknowledgments
We would like to thank the following for permission to
reproduce photographs: Getty Images: Mint Images, 26;
iStockphotos: © GJohnson2, 22; Photoshot: Jeff Simon,
18; Shutterstock: ANDRZEJ GRZEGORCZYK, 16,
Audrey Snider-Bell, 25, Cathy Keifer, 12, CreativeNature.
nl, 27, David Evison, 20, 28, Delmas Lehman, 11, Heiko
Kiera, 19, holbox, 10, Jonald Morales, 15, Kjeld Friis, 7,
Kjersti Joergensen, 21, Leena Robinson, 13, 29 Bottom,
leungchopan, Cover, Linda Bucklin, 24, Matt Jeppson, 6,
Maxim Petrichuk, 4, Melinda Fawver, 17, Morris Mann, 8,
PhotoSky, Design Element, Raffaella Calzoni, 5,
worldswildlifewonders, 14; SuperStock: Animals Animals,
23, 29 Middle, Tier und Naturfotografie, 9, 29 Top.

We would like to thank Michael Bright for his invaluable
help in the preparation of this book.

Every effort has been made to contact copyright holders
of material reproduced in this book. Any omissions will
be rectified in subsequent printings if notice is given to
the publisher.

All the Internet addresses (URLs) given in this book were
valid at the time of going to press. However, due to the
dynamic nature of the Internet, some addresses may have
changed, or sites may have changed or ceased to exist since
publication. While the author and publisher regret any
inconvenience this may cause readers, no responsibility for
any such changes can be accepted by either the author or
the publisher.

Contents

APR 2 0 2015

Some words are shown in bold, **like this**. You can find out what they mean by looking in the glossary.

Meet the Reptiles

Reptiles are a large group of animals that includes lizards, snakes, turtles, alligators, and crocodiles. Scientists divide living things into groups. This is called **classification**.

Many lizards live in hot places. They even live in deserts.

Alligators live in rivers and swamps. Watch out for their sharp teeth!

Each group is different from other groups in particular ways. All reptiles have dry skin, which is covered in **scales**, and they keep warm by taking in heat from their surroundings.

5

Body Shape

Reptiles belong to a larger group of animals called **vertebrates**. Like humans and other **mammals**, they have a **skeleton** made of bones. Their backbone is made of many smaller, knobby bones.

A snake has a very long backbone!

A turtle swims by using its legs as paddles or flippers to pull it through the water.

Most reptiles have four legs, which they use to move on land and in water. Snakes have no legs. They move by bending their bodies into an "S" shape and pushing back against the ground.

Long, Bending Snakes

Snakes use their long, bendable bodies in many ways. They **coil** up their bodies to rest and to sleep. Tree snakes wind and slither through the branches of trees.

A tree snake coils its body over a branch.

Anacondas can grow to long lengths.

Snakes such as pythons and anacondas wrap their bodies around **prey** and then squeeze them to death. Other snakes kill their prey with **venom**, which they inject through their **fangs**.

Warming Up

Most reptiles are **cold-blooded**. This means that they cannot make their own heat, as birds and **mammals** do. Instead, they take in heat from their surroundings.

A lizard warms up quickly by basking in the sunshine.

An alligator may slide into the river to cool down on a hot day.

When reptiles are cold, they move very slowly. As they warm up, they move around much faster. In parts of the world with cold winters, many reptiles make a **burrow** and **hibernate**.

Lizards

Lizards like hot places and many live in deserts. Once they have warmed up they move fast, catching insects to eat. If they get too hot, they move into the shade or under a rock to cool down.

This chameleon has an extremely long tongue for catching insects.

tongue

This green anole is a lizard. It can change the color of its skin to match its surroundings.

Many lizards are brightly colored. Some lizards blend in with their surroundings. This is called **camouflage**. They may also change color when they are angry!

Scaly Skin

A reptile's skin is covered with hard **scales**. The scales are waterproof and stop the reptile's body from drying out. Crocodiles have large, heavy scales, but lizards and snakes have much smaller ones.

A crocodile has a tough, thick skin. Its back is protected by hard plates, like armor.

A snake's skin can have different colors and patterns.

The scales on a snake's skin do not grow as the snake grows. When the skin gets too small, the snake wriggles out of it, revealing a new skin underneath.

Turtles and Tortoises

Turtles and tortoises are even better protected than crocodiles. The skin is covered with thick **scales,** which join together to make the shell that you see.

A giant tortoise measures up to 4 feet (1.2 meters) long.

A tortoise's shell is smooth and shiny.

Tortoises and some turtles can pull their legs and head into the shell. Then their whole body is protected.

Laying Eggs

A reptile begins life inside an egg. Some reptiles make a hole in the ground, like a nest, and lay their eggs in it. Most reptiles' eggs have a bendable, leathery shell, but crocodiles, tortoises, and some geckos lay eggs with hard shells.

American alligators lay their eggs in a mound of rotting plants.

This young python is beginning to hatch.

A baby reptile has a special egg tooth. When it is ready to **hatch**, the baby uses its egg tooth to cut its way out of the shell.

Baby Turtles

Although turtles live in the ocean, they lay their eggs on land. The mother turtle lays her eggs on a beach, out of reach of the sea. She covers them with sand before she returns to the sea.

A female turtle digs a hole in the sand for her eggs.

Lots of baby turtles hatch at the same time. They run across the sand to reach the sea.

When the eggs **hatch,** the tiny turtles rush down the beach to the sea. Many are snapped up by hungry birds before they reach the water.

Young Reptiles

Most young reptiles have to take care of themselves from the moment they **hatch**. Only a few survive to become adults. The rest are caught by **predators**, such as birds and other reptiles.

Young baby snakes have to find their own food and try to avoid being eaten.

These baby alligators ride safely through the water on their mother's head!

Crocodiles and alligators take care of their young. When young Nile crocodiles hatch, their mother carries them in her mouth to the water.

Great Survivors

Reptiles have survived on Earth for a very long time. Dinosaurs were reptiles and were the most powerful animals on Earth for millions of years.

Stegosaurus lived about 150 million years ago. It ate plants and had two rows of bony plates on its back.

Crocodiles first appeared on Earth about 250 million years ago.

Many reptiles that lived at the same time as the dinosaurs died out about 64 million years ago. Crocodiles did not die out and have changed very little.

One Amazing Reptile!

Tuataras live in the wild on islands off the coast of New Zealand. They have lived on Earth for about 200 million years, almost as long as crocodiles. Tuataras look like lizards, but they are **classified** in a group of their own.

A tuatara is the only living member of its group.

A tuatara has a row of spines along its back.

Tuataras grow very slowly. Young tuataras have a mysterious third eye on top of their heads. It becomes covered by **scales** as they grow into adults.

Quiz

Look at the pictures below and read the clues. Can you remember the names of these reptiles? Look back in the book if you need help.

1. I live in the ocean but lay my eggs on a sandy beach. What am I?

Answers
1. turtle
2. anaconda
3. baby alligator
4. green anole

28

2. I squeeze my **prey** to death. I can grow very long. What am I?

3. I am a baby and my mother takes care of me. What am I?

4. The color of my skin changes to match my surroundings. What am I?

Glossary

burrow animal's underground home

camouflage when the color or shape of an animal causes it to blend in with its surroundings

classification system that scientists use to divide living things into separate groups

classified put into a group according to special things shared by that group

coil wind around and around in a circle

cold-blooded when an animal is unable to make its own heat and has to take heat from its surroundings

fang long, hollow tooth

hatch break out of an egg

hibernate go into a very deep sleep to survive very cold or very dry weather

mammal animal that has hair and feeds its young with milk from the mother

predator animal that kills other animals for food

prey animal that is hunted by another animal for food

scales small, hard plates that cover an animal's skin

skeleton hard frame that gives vertebrate animals their shape

venom poison that is injected by a sting or bite

vertebrate animal that has a backbone and skeleton inside its body

Find Out More

Books

Berger, Melvin and Gilda. *Reptiles* (True or False). New York: Scholastic, 2008.

Clarke, Catriona. *Reptiles* (Usborne Beginners). Tulsa, Okla.: EDC, 2009.

Schuetz, Kari. *Reptiles* (Blastoff!: Animal Classes). Minneapolis: Bellwether, 2013.

Thomas, Isabel. *Remarkable Reptiles* (Extreme Animals). Chicago: Raintree, 2013.

Web sites

FactHound offers a safe, fun way to find internet sites related to this book. All of the sites on FactHound have been researched by our staff.

Here's all you do:
Visit www.facthound.com
Type in this code: 9781484607541

Index